Ten Poems about Bicycles

Candlestick Press

Published by:
Candlestick Press,
21, Devonshire Avenue, Beeston,
Nottingham NG9 1BS, UK
Tel: 07500 180871
www.candlestickpress.co.uk

Typeset and printed by Parker and Collinson Ltd.
Nottingham NG7 2FH
Tel: 0115 942 0140
www.parkerandcollinson.co.uk

Cover and book-plate illustration: © Rosalind Bliss, 2009
Candlestick Press monogram: © Barbara Shaw, 2008
Introduction: © Jenny Swann, 2009

© Candlestick Press, 2009
Reprinted 2010

ISBN 978 0 9558944 5 9

Acknowledgements:
The publisher acknowledges with thanks the estate of Michael Donaghy and Pan Macmillan, London, for permission to print 'Machines' from *Remembering Dances Learned Last Night*, Picador, 2000; Paul McLoughlin and Shoestring Press for permission to print 'The Bicycle Garden', from *What Moves Moves*, Shoestring Press, 2004; Helena Nelson for 'Bike with no hands', from *Starlight on Water*, The Rialto; James Roderick Burns and *Fire* for permission to print 'Boy on a Bicycle'; Jonathan Davidson for 'A Lady Cyclist Learns To Cycle' from *Moving the Stereo*, Jackson's Arm, 1993; Connie Bensley and Bloodaxe Books for 'Wheel Fever' from *Choosing to be a Swan*, Bloodaxe Books, 1994, the estate of the late Phyllis Flowerdew (Noel Kingsbury) for permission to use 'A Spider Bought a Bicycle'. Derek Mahon, 'The Bicycle', is from *Collected Poems* (1999) by kind permission of the author and The Gallery Press. The publisher has used every endeavour to contact Coney for permission to use the haiku posted on www.bikeforums.net and reproduced here on the back cover.

Note: where poets are no longer living, their dates are given.

Introduction

The bicycle is a wonderful example of benign technology. Loved and eulogised by all who ride them, bicycles remind us of freedom, speed, the space to think our own thoughts. For the technically-minded, they are a paradise of valves, pumps and sprockets, their history amounting to a paean to the ball-bearing.

The claims made for bicycles are many and magnificent. In the latter half of the twentieth century, it was said that 'socialism can only arrive by bicycle' (contemporary politicians might wish to debate that one) while earlier in the century, the writer John Galsworthy credited bicycles with nothing less than the emancipation of women.

Ten Poems about Bicycles covers as many different aspects of the bicycle as is possible in so short a space, from its early history, through some teething problems – mostly in the brakes department – on to the affection that bicycles have inspired in their riders, and the miraculous and sometimes poignant associations that have gathered around them in poetry.

Jenny Swann,
Editor

Mulga Bill's Bicycle

'TWAS Mulga Bill, from Eaglehawk, that caught the cycling craze:
He turned away the good old horse that served him many days;
He dressed himself in cycling clothes, resplendent to be seen;
He hurried off to town and bought a shining new machine;
And as he wheeled it through the door, with air of lordly pride,
The grinning shop assistant said, 'Excuse me, can you ride?' .

'See here, young man,' said Mulga Bill, 'from Walgett to the sea,
From Conroy's Gap to Castlereagh, there's none can ride like me.
I'm good all round at everything, as everybody knows,
Although I'm not the one to talk - I hate a man that blows.
But riding is my special gift, my chiefest, sole delight;
Just ask a wild duck can it swim, a wild cat can it fight.
There's nothing clothed in hair or hide, or built of flesh or steel,
There's nothing walks or jumps, or runs, on axle, hoof or wheel,
But what I'll sit, while hide will hold and girths and straps are tight;
I'll ride this here two-wheeled concern right straight away at sight.'

'Twas Mulga Bill, from Eaglehawk, that sought his own abode,
That perched above the Dead Man's Creek, beside the mountain road.
He turned the cycle down the hill and mounted for the fray,
But ere he'd gone a dozen yards it bolted clean away.
It left the track, and through the trees, just like a silver streak,
It whistled down the awful slope towards the Dead Man's Creek.

It shaved a stump by half an inch, it dodged a big white-box:
The very wallaroos in fright went scrambling up the rocks,
The wombats hiding in their caves dug deeper underground,
But Mulga Bill, as white as chalk, clung tight to every bound.

It struck a stone and gave a spring that cleared a fallen tree,
It raced beside a precipice as close as close could be;
And then, as Mulga Bill let out one last despairing shriek,
It made a leap of twenty feet into the Dead Man's Creek.

'Twas Mulga Bill, from Eaglehawk, that slowly swam ashore:
He said, 'I've had some narrer shaves and lively rides before;
I've rode a wild bull round a yard to win a five-pound bet,
But that was sure the derndest ride that I've encountered yet.
I'll give that two-wheeled outlaw best; it's shaken all my nerve
To feel it whistle through the air and plunge and buck and swerve.
It's safe at rest in Dead Man's Creek - we'll leave it lying still;
A horse's back is good enough henceforth for Mulga Bill.'

Andrew Barton 'Banjo' Paterson (1864 – 1941)

Wheel Fever

Frank Reynolds has ordered a Coventry,
48 inches high and with all
the new improvements.

But it cost £14, and I am afraid
to sink so much money - it would be almost
three months of my salary.

All the fellows in the village
have bicycle fever, and none
more than myself.

*

Rode on Aubrey's wooden cycle
into Warboys, to see a Spider-Wheel
which Monty has for sale.

But the tyres were tied on
with pieces of twine, so I did not
part with my cash.

*

I've done it! I could not bear to wait
any longer. I now possess a Coventry
(without the new improvements).

Before I paid, I took it for a spin
but lost the treadle,
landed in a heap

and had to have it taken back
in the cart, and put together.
But after that

I rode off round the lanes
as right as twelve o'clock
and pleased as Punch.

*

Coming back from a spin today, I met
Mr Dodds with his cartload of bread.
He must have known

that horses shy at bicycles, but
he did not get down, and sure enough
his wretched animal

reared, backed into the dyke, and emptied
22 stone of bread and 6 stone of flour
into the water.

*

Set out with James Black, to ride
to the prayer meeting, but
by Redman's corner

he ran into me, knocked me off,
broke my handle, bent my treadle, and fell
on top of me.

*

I am receiving unpleasant letters from
Mr Dodds. I do not believe that flour
can be so dear.

Unlike Aubrey or Frank Reynolds,
I can now ride my bicycle
with arms folded.

    *

I was riding my bicycle with my arms
folded on my way to Doddington,
when I hit a stone

and pitched on my head. Managed to get up
and stagger on, covered with blood
and feeling faint.

Of course I could not help Uncle
in the shop. The carrier put his pony in
and took me home.

    *

Could not move this morning, so stiff
and sore. My bicycle will take three days
to put right.

I miss it dreadfully. Frank Reynolds
does not seem keen on the idea
of lending me his.

But I have had a carrot poultice put on
my eye and I shall soon be fit enough
to ride again.

Connie Bensley

Boy on a Bicycle

A boy rides a bicycle before the first world war. He is eighteen, almost nineteen - a man, really - and wears his new uniform with pride. He is cycling along an embankment on the outskirts of a small town. The sun is halfway towards noon, the wind tousling his light brown hair; his pinkish lips are mouthing a music-hall ditty under his sparse moustache. He is going to see a girl he used to know.

He has no idea he will be dead in a week, his legs thrown out the wrong way under a snarl of barbed wire. Now he marvels at the warmth of his muscles as the chain drives the wheels around. Now his tongue tastes of mint and apples.

James Roderick Burns

A Lady Cyclist Learns to Cycle

(England, 1917)

They led it round the yard and garden
on a long rein.
They fed it oil.

It was black as my jet black boots,
heavy as a gate.
It ticked, shone.

Climbing on it, I felt it shy,
lunge beneath me,
clatter to earth.

They held me up, the men, laughing,
shouldered me round,
gentlemanly.

The guns of Passchendaele bellowed.
The men held me.
It shook, I shook,

but when they let go, I did not
let go, but moved
forward, shouting.

Jonathan Davidson

The Bicycle

There was a bicycle, a fine
Raleigh with five gears
And racing handlebars.
It stood at the front door
Begging to be mounted;
The frame shone in the sun.

I became like a character
In *The Third Policeman*, half
Human, half bike, my life
A series of dips and ridges,
Happiness a free-wheeling
Past fragrant hawthorn hedges.

Cape and sou'wester streamed
With rain as I rode to school
Side-tracking the bus routes.
Night after night I dreamed
Of valves, pumps, sprockets,
Reflectors and repair kits.

Soon there were long rides
In the country, wet weekends
Playing cards in the kitchens
Of mountain youth hostels,
Day-runs to Monaghan,
Rough and exotic roads.

It went with me to Dublin
Where I sold it the same winter;
But its wheels still sing
In the memory, stars that turn
About an eternal centre,
The bright spokes glittering.

Derek Mahon

Bike with no Hands

One look at you and I knew
you'd be able to ride a bike with no hands.

I tried it, of course, but could never do it.
It was written all over your face that you
would have practised, bare legs, bloody knees,
in the summer evenings, hours at a time
when no-one was watching the mishaps, until
casually, coolly, at infinite ease,
you'd ride, no-handed, surveying the street,
as if you'd been born on a circus bike.

I wish - but then, we are what we are.
I drive with two hands, walk with both feet
firmly planted on sensible ground. And
I've got you. You can ride with no hands.

Helena Nelson

Machines

Dearest, note how these two are alike:
This harpsichord pavane by Purcell
And the racer's twelve-speed bike.

The machinery of grace is always simple.
This chrome trapezoid, one wheel connected
To another of concentric gears,
Which Ptolemy dreamt of and Schwinn perfected,
Is gone. The cyclist, not the cycle, steers.
And in the playing, Purcell's chords are played away.

So this talk, or touch if I were there,
Should work its effortless gadgetry of love,
Like Dante's heaven, and melt into the air.

If it doesn't, of course, I've fallen. So much is chance,
So much agility, desire, and feverish care,
As bicyclists and harpsichordists prove

Who only by moving can balance,
Only by balancing move.

Michael Donaghy (1954 - 2004)

The Bicycle Garden

The graves of children who go missing
are abandoned bicycles set in concrete
bases lowered into shallow trenches
by the railway bridge and left to rust.
The engineer (retired) who tends
the place says visitors are few -
he imagines parents driving slowly by
or peering through the wire-mesh fence
for a particular shade of paint or rake
of handlebar, but they don't come in.

And there it was, this gaunt tableau
of BMXs, racers, mountain bikes,
an aged Vespa with its fairing crushed,
and tricycles with tassels tied to handle grips
or crossbars, where they stayed, seeming,
to those who looked, to rise up from the ground
or sink into it. You turn away -

because there's no such garden, though
the bicycles are often all that's found.
An end-page columnist invented it
when it seemed to him society
was waging war on being young,
on children who enticed and let you
down. So he dreamed a garden for them,
and the engineer was somehow odd
enough to make the whole thing real,
a sleight that left its maker lying
with the silence in his ears, as if
some violence had been done.

Paul McLoughlin

A Spider Bought a Bicycle

A spider bought a bicycle
And had it painted black
He started off along the road
With an earwig on his back
He sent the pedals round so fast
He travelled all the day
Then he took the earwig off
And put the bike away.

Phyllis Flowerdew (1913-1994)